Larceny

Jazmin Galloway

Copyright © 2023 by Jazmin Galloway

All rights reserved.

ISBN – 978-1-7351652-7-1

LOC – 9781735165271

10 9 8 7 6 5 4 3 2 1

No portion of this book may be reproduced in any form without written permission from the publisher or author, except as permitted by U.S. copyright law. All characters, names, places, and events mentioned in this book are a part of the author's imagination and in no way reflect, or replicate real people, events, or places.

Trigger Warnings
- ~Depression
- ~Mentions of self-harm and harming others
- ~Lots of unfiltered emotions
- ~Miscarriage and childbirth
- ~Murder, Loss, and Grieving

To all my fears.

WE ARE ALL JUST trying to live.

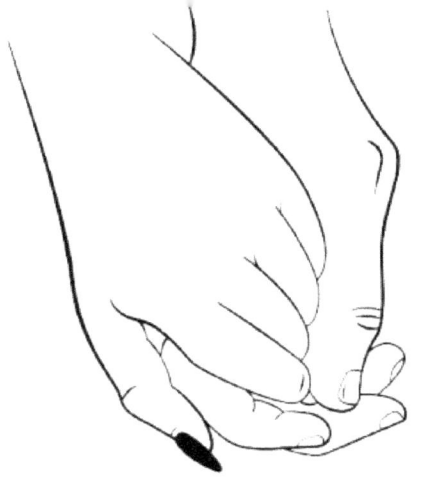

DEATH

Three drops of ink on
white paper

Smudged
Streaked
Stripped-bare
Ineligible words of warfare

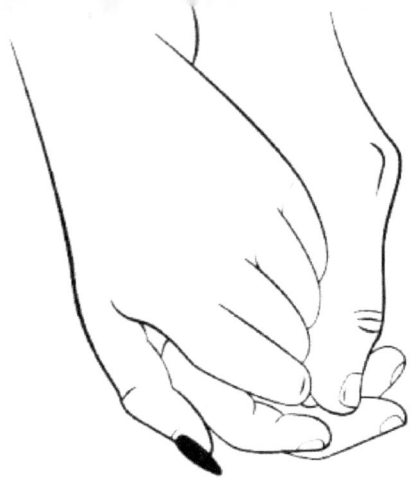

Purpose

I SUPPOSE ITS PURPOSE
    is direct
    5 words 1 line
    the cause of death.

    Unspoken, unchosen
    But simply true
    Eyes Of Knives laid on you

    I suppose its purpose
    Is a threat
    5 words 1 one
    One last breath.

    Purposely written
    But laid to rest
    A desire,
    A fire,

A resilient breath

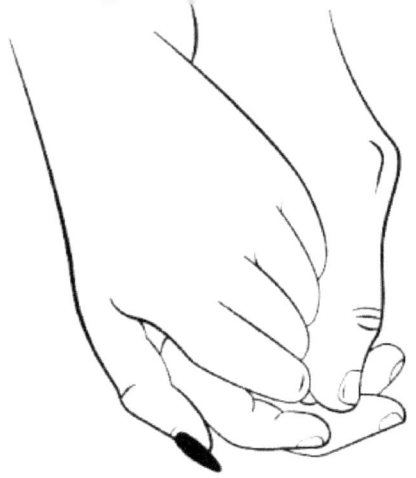

Breathe

Breath
   in
   Then
   out

   Shaking hands
   Wobbling knees

   Breathe
   in
   Then
   out

   Tease, please,
   kiss, and knead

   Bleed
   in

Then
out

Until there isn't enough
left to bleed.

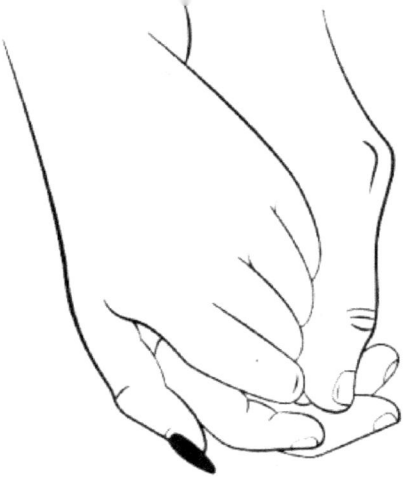

BLEED

RED ROSES WILTING IN your cloudy water,
Bubbles disintegrating in its milky stare,
Blood dripping from your glossy hair

Yet you
don't bleed,
like me.

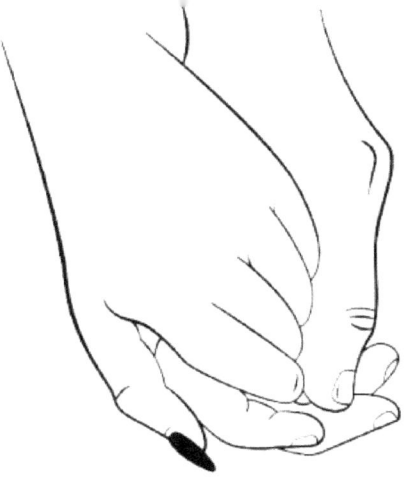

ROSES

IN A VASE UNDER the window
   Posed like a child does a doll,

  Sitting, wilting, still
  Broken, frozen, ill

  Ill to the touch
  Lost in its warmth
  Driven
   mad by its
   bad by its
  Passion.

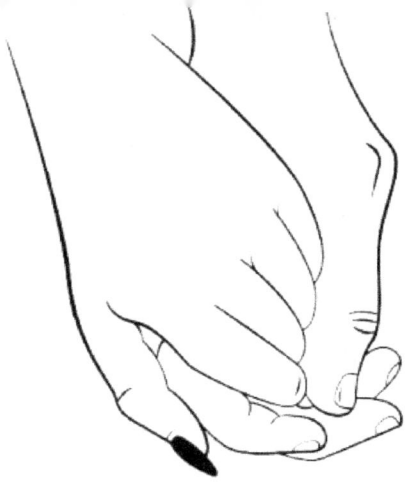

Passion

AFFECTIONATE KISSES
   Broken glass
   Soft whimpers
   A lost plead
   NO
   Fumbling hands
   Raising pressure,
   a reason to scream.

   A silent home
   Take me home, please

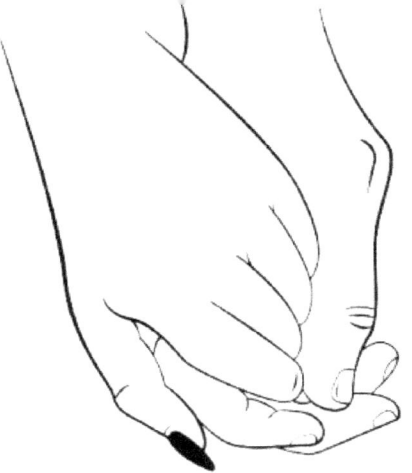

HOME

A THUMPING
    A bumping
    A knock
    Heavy steps softened to a trot
    Unsettling tick-tock from the clock
    Un-dreaming eyes glued to the sky
    A stray tear from eye to ear
    A sinking gut,
    a numbing look
    In the doorway stands a monster.

MONSTER

YOUR GUARDIAN KNOWS BEST
But it's what they do not know
Your guardian knows best
It's what I cannot tell

That a monster in the shape of a man
Used his hand
To take away my voice.

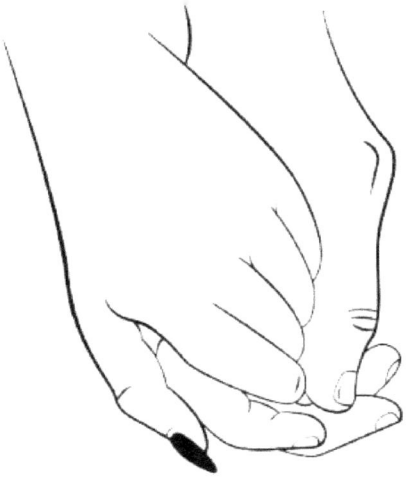

My Voice

I'm in a place that makes me scared,
    Of where I am going
    And what I will share

    Heard when I'm quiet
    Unheard when I am loud

    Beaten
    Bruised
    Bolted down

    Grappled
    Stretched
    Thrown

    Into the air
    Then back down

Jostled by life's changing mind
Like a mind in a mime
field

Mime Field

Chasing ever-changing
  faces, painted, breaking
  Down into dust
  Like atoms of
  MAN

  Chasing death
  Like a mule does its fuel
  Pacing breath
  'Til
  Death
  Do us part.

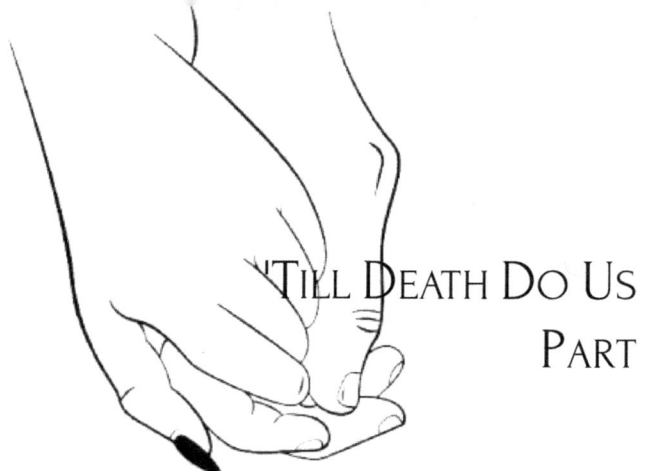

'Till Death Do Us Part

Woven together
 Your limbs on mine
 A blur of color and fabric.

A taste of you before
A taste of you now
A taste of you later

An elixir of life to soak my tongue in
A breath of air to swallow me whole
A moment of time to take you in
I hope I hold
'Til death do us part.

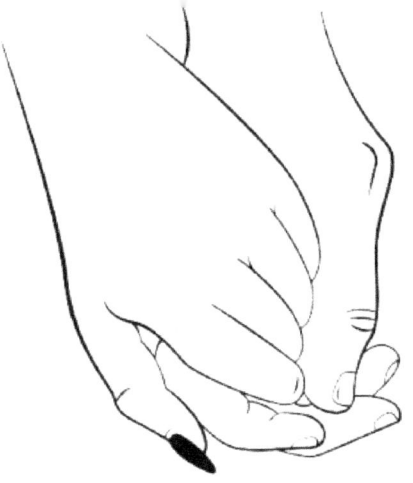

WOVEN

THREADED
   Embedded
   Sprinkled throughout the room

   A split bat
   A misshapen hat
   And shoes to match

   Cloud like fabric gathered in a tomb
   Hidden from sight,
   Yet not hiding

   Woven in the details,
   Unopened.

UNOPENED

5 WORDS 1 LINE

Smoothed on pink stationery
Immaculately placed on a pillow
Shrouded in clouds

A ghost of memories
Touching its grounds
Tucked away in a crinkling   envelope
To never be found

Unopened.

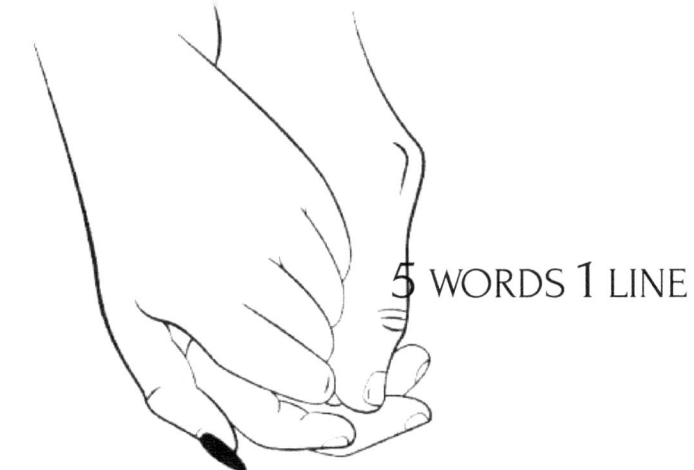

5 WORDS 1 LINE

I WISH YOU WOULD die

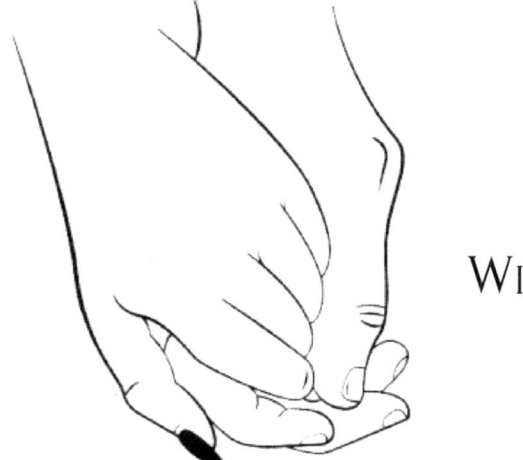

WISHING

Crack
Chatter
Splatter
on to the floor

Wishing nothing more
than what you deserve
Oddly enough
It's not enough
to snuff
out
your memory

Your touching, pleading, grieving,
Your eyes, smile, lips
What I would give
to wish

for you
again.

LARCENY

Love
    Altering
    Reality
    Circles
    Every
    New
    Youth

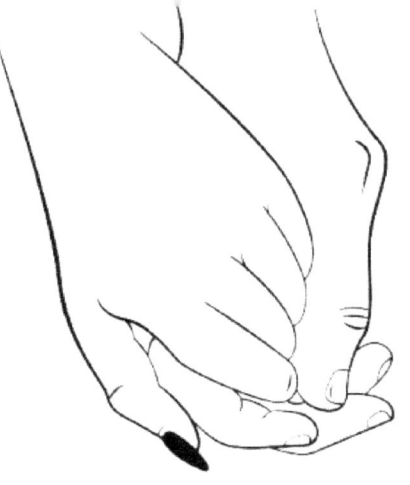

LOVE

EVEN WHEN MY EYES are closed
   I still feel your presence near

   Growing, holding, festering,

   UNDER my skin
   But not unwelcome

   Just unpleasantly molding
   ~~me~~ us
   to your liking.

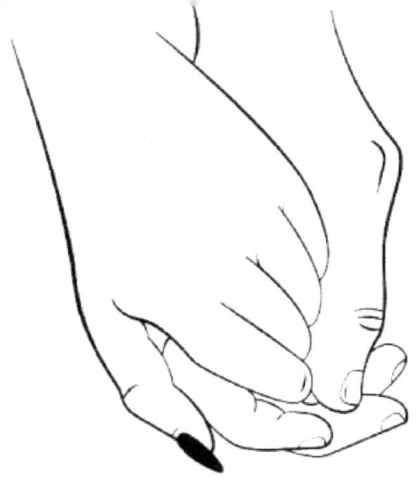

ALTERING

MOLDING
    Warping
    Configure
    whatever is done

    Triggers

    My inner conscience
    My mental battalion

    Why me?
    How can I...?

    let you
    change me
    alter my mind
    take my heart.

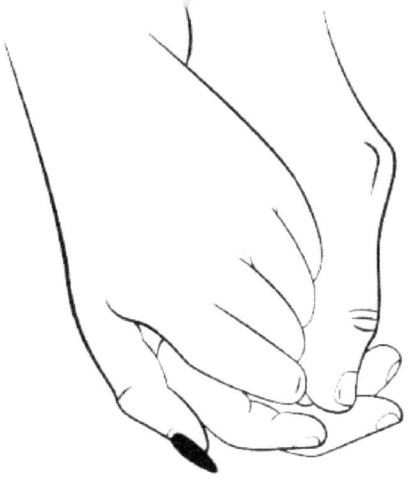

REALITY

BASK IN THE GLOW
   of your mistakes
   Make it better
   tomorrow

   A fantasy isn't reality

   It makes you
   hazy and lazy
   light and dazed

   It feels like a dream

   And in my dreams you are not allowed
through.
   Though,
   you creep,
   you wander,

you arrive

Inside of my mind.

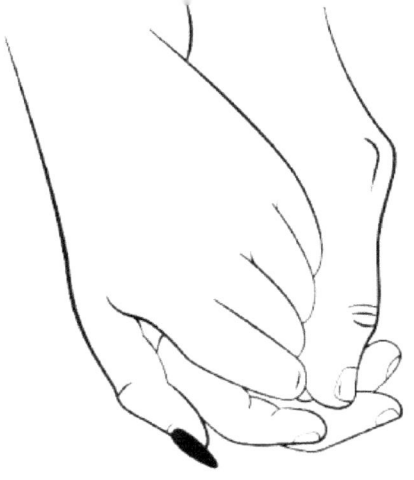

CIRCLES

Repetitious loops
    360 degrees
    over and over
    I stumble
    into you

    Your arms open and pouring
    emotion, towards me
    Choking me under its clouds

    A fog in a misty rain forest

    Thick and inhabitable
    but it feels habitable
    So I enter
    My silhouette shadowed by your **darkness**

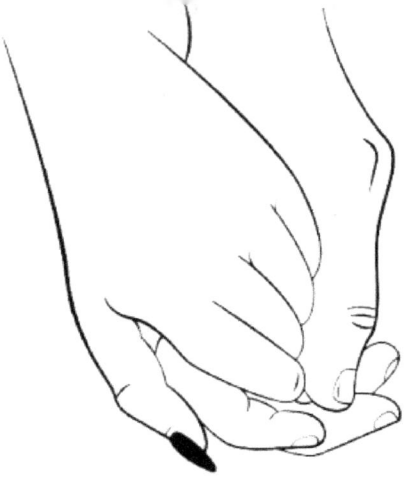

EVERY

EVERY BREATH,
    Every touch,
    Every smile,
    Every word,
    Chosen specifically for me.

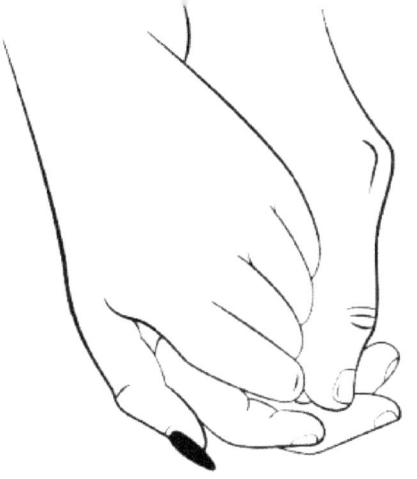

New

Small breaths of hot air
   Tiny fingers, and tiny toes
   Watery eyes, a pink nose
   A babe.

   Young and fun
   Joyous and plump
   Innocent to life's mysteries.

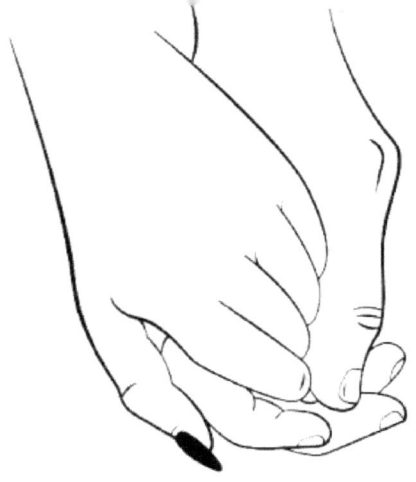

YOUTH

INNOCENCE
- Watermelon slices
- Swaying trees
- Sharp grass
- Laughter
- The sun
- Father's call

Father's Call

A ringing phone.
   Unread texts.
   Police report .
   Yellow tape.
   Flashing cameras.
   Blood.
   5 words 1 line
   Written on pink stationery.

Freedom Calls

Like death
   It coddles you in a tight embrace
   An ode to life

   Whisking away innocence in place of
   Freedom

   To dream

        uninhibited

   To touch

        without pain

   To scream

        into the morning sun

Freedom's call
ringing through the walls
like an unanswered phone.

Life's Love

Mother's touch has always been
Perfect
Soft, and sweet
Singular, unique.

To give to her
Is to receive
Cherishing the moments that she
B r e a t h e s

Though her blue eyes are not mine
and
her smile reminds me
of **him**

She's divine
and free
because

of **me**

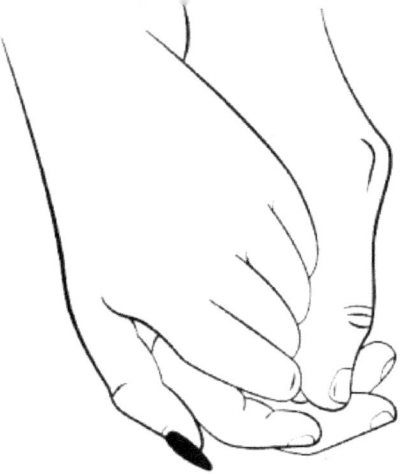

RISE

A RISING OF
    insecurity
    fear
    worry
    pain
    memory
    loss

    A need to
    leave
    pray
    cry
    scream
    punish

    RUN

    5 words 1 line

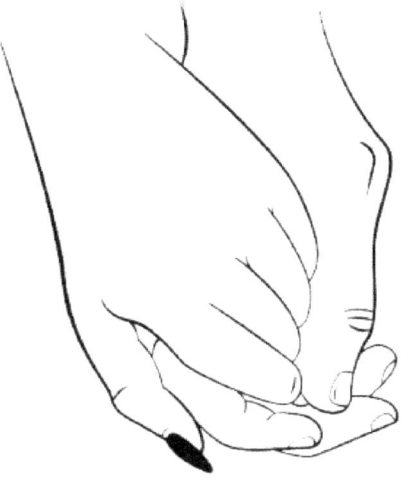

Theft

IN THE NIGHT
   you stole my mind
   here you are
   after some time

   Translucent

   and a part of the *w i n d*

   Here you are
   evermore

   A part of me, taken
   A part of you, taken

   A theft of youth
   For a theft of life

Possession

IT COMES TO ME like a memory
my silhouette emerging from your darkness

TALL
Proud
Changed

Yet,
somehow you linger
behind the lids of my eyes
in a darkened form
head split open
eyes wide open
mouth
wide
Open

Possessing me

Inside, your words burn
not tangible
but burying deep
unbridled anger
resentment
pain
Weighing me down
S l o w i n g my walk
to freedom

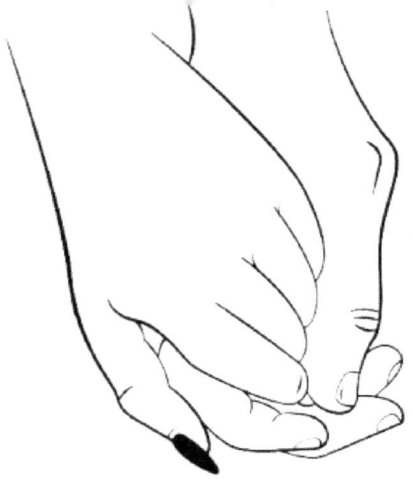

GRUDGE

WARFARE
 Isn't fair.
 If one cries
 The other
 must die
 repay the debts
 that are due.
 If you do not hold,
 the grudge will hold you.

Mother's Call

Time flies when you're having fun
   Children grow when you're having fun
   Secrets dull when you're having fun

   Mother calls
   and I answer.
   At first, silence.

   Then a whisper
   a plea
   an address
   a theft of freedom

   Take me home, please

Silver Cuffs

5 WORDS 1 LINE
   and a signed note

   A split bat
   A misshapen hat
   And shoes to match

   A reason to scream
   Take me home, please

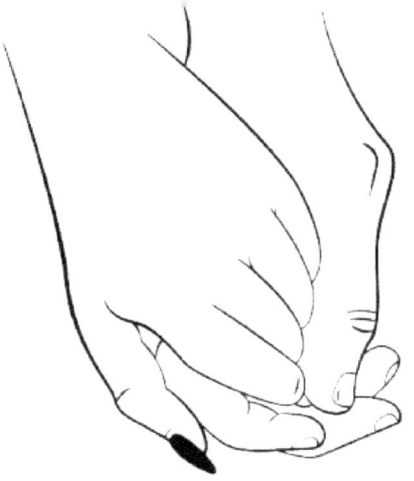

DECAY

WASTING AWAY
    locked in a pen
    like a hen
    cold without hay
    causing decay
    rotten to the core
    knowing no more,
    than **them**

Stripped-Bare

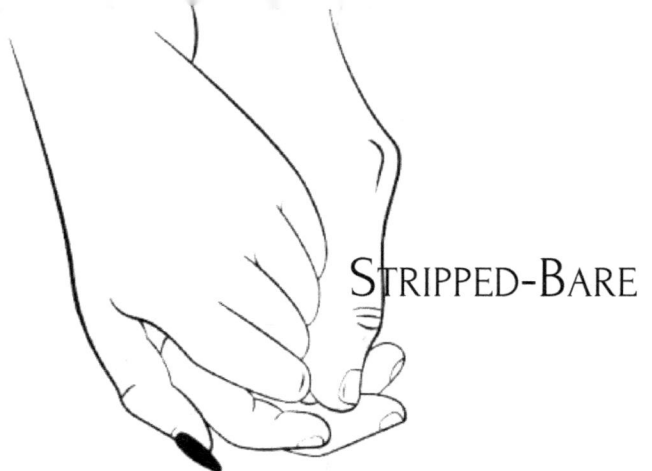

Photos
- Clothes
- Weapons
- Gold
- Money
- Madness
- Lies

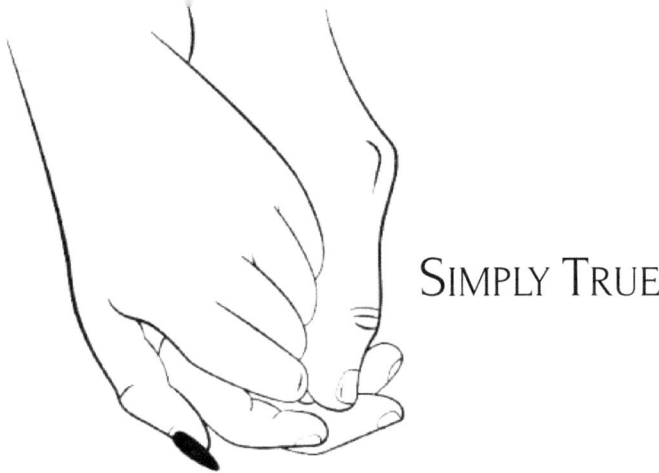

Simply True

5 WORDS 1 LINE
meant to stay unopened
Yet, the person who was chosen
never went to open
the letter.

So here it sits
under boiling yellow light
alight to the public eye
Tears spring to her eyes

Because it's simply true,
you get what you wish for.

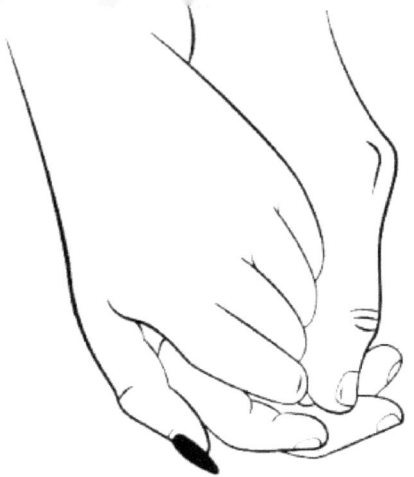

Alibi

THAT DATE
    a glorious occasion
    Where love circles youth
    The birth of her babe
    saves
    her from decay
    and rotting away
    for good.

For the day
her babe was born
she was torn
from the scene of the crime.

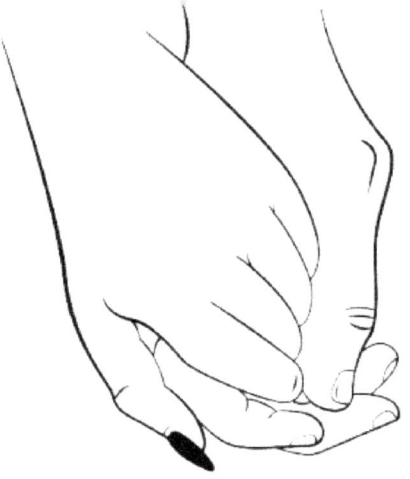

Property

Mind numbing sights
A broken home
A series of fights
Streaks of blood on shiny hardwood floors
But,
silence
brings tears of joy.
Home,
at last.

REINVENTION

RE-TILE THE FLOORS,
    Repaint the walls,
    Sweep up the glass,
    Toss the gauze,
    Mop up the blood.
    Fix it all.

A Transit

Shifting energy brings air to my lungs
   water to my faucet
   and words to my tongue.

   Shifting energy brings money to my bank
   family to my home
   and sends looks my way.

   Shifting energy brings normalcy to my daughter
   food to the table
   and flowers to the altar.

   A shift in energy brings a new him
   to me

A Father For My Daughter

AT FIRST GLANCE
    my daughter needs no father
    just lessons taught by her mother

    Though there are things a mother cannot teach,
    a way to see the world that is indeed unique
    Words of encouragement
    or just words at all
    that a mother won't utter
    ones that cause her to shutter
    blink rapidly and stutter.

    A father for my daughter
    is what he will be.
    A man with a mind and heart
    that lets mother breathe.

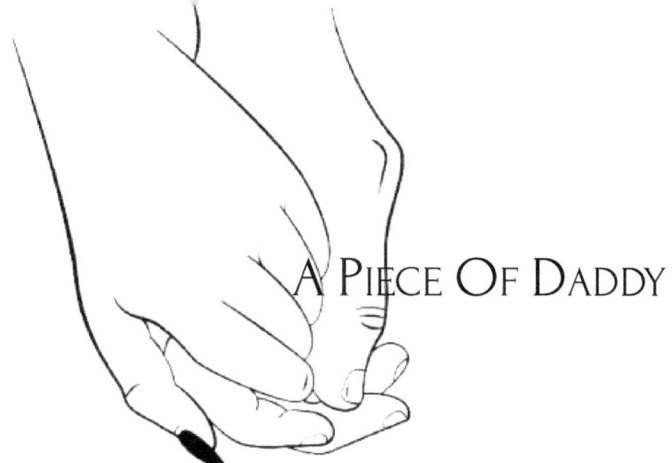

A Piece Of Daddy

A blood curling scream
   cannot describe
   the sound I made
   at my daughter's find
   It was dry, crusted, bloody and dirty
   but the same blue reflected in my daughter's
   eyes

   A piece of Daddy, placed in a shoe
   right inside the room
   where we
   made
   you.

And There It Goes

THERE GOES THE PEACE
mother has created

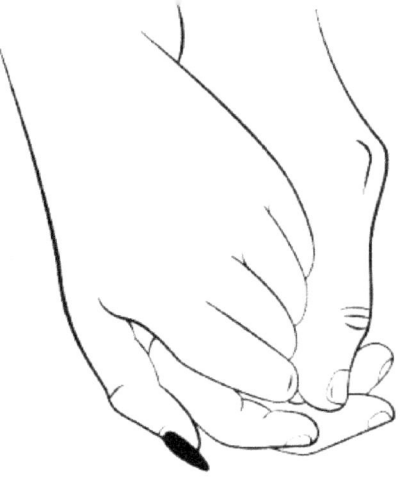

PEACE

AFTER MANY YEARS HE has risen
  not dead or alive, but an admission.
  A man not gone
  and a man not far
  Opening wounds that were once scars
  Taking away the peace of the night
  Heavy minds that ponder fright
  Leaving homes, taking flight,
  Away into the sun once again.

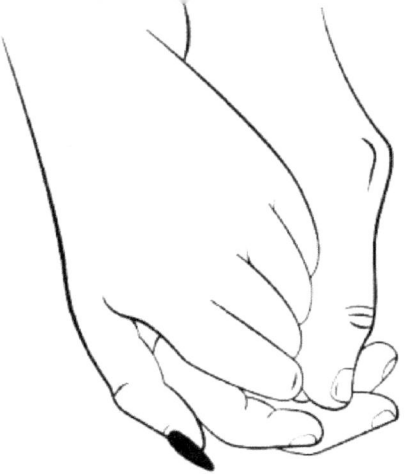

THREAT

A SEARCH GIVES WAY to a brittle note
written to a woman who once did know
the secret that lies between jilted lovers.
Left for others to uncover
and for a cowering mother to rediscover
The woman who made her suffer.

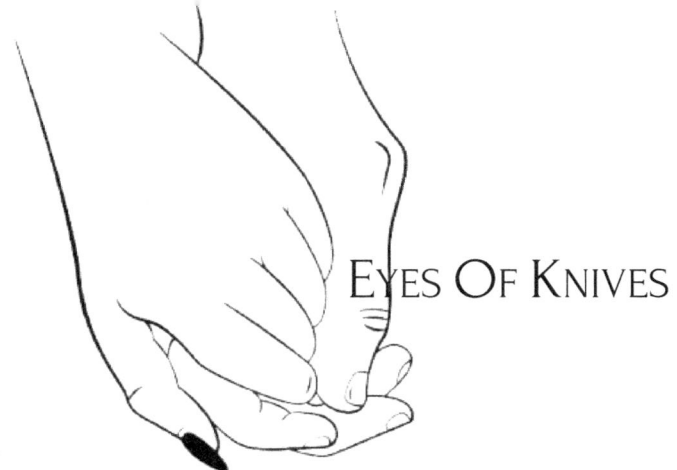

Eyes Of Knives

BEHIND HER BACK SHE checks;
   memories from the past

   Who is this dreaded woman?
   Which fear has amassed

   What does she gain by torture?
   And what will she do?

   Better yet,
   who
   will
   she
   choose?

A Woman, A Gun, A Wish

ON A DARK, RAINY night
   a soul sweeps in on the wind
   hushed, quiet, and unafraid.

   'Kin' cannot describe who this soul is
   'Friend' does not describe who this soul is
   'Enemy' can only say what this soul has become.

   Wandering from town to town
   with a loaded gun
   Hair black like night
   and eyes of knives
   Erupting from the shadows with one wish.

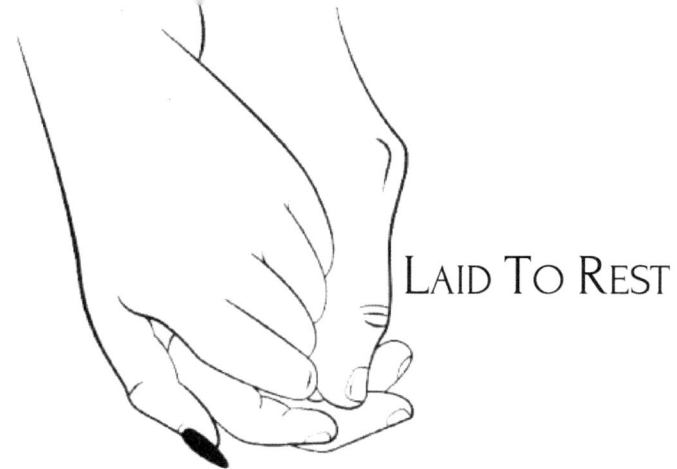

Laid To Rest

I DID NOT MEAN to make you cry
   I took a life from you
   now, you take mine

   Like a monster,
   in the doorway you creep
   A fuzzy rug,
   softens your feet
   Metal cool in your hands
   goes warm
   when you pull the trigger

   Your gun **jams**

   And I wake,
   to your *burning* eyes
   It's no surprise
   you'd try to rob me of my life

Black Petals On A White Coffin

Dressed in black from head to toe
   A mourning mother I used to know
   A grieving father full of rage
   Another incident
   CENTER STAGE
   A plea of self-defense
   with footage to match

              A trial dropped

              A sentence stopped

   Another down lightning fast
   Gone like a wish on the wind
   As her soul had wandered in

Dropping black petals,
on a white casket.

No Place Is Safe

Everywhere the woman walks,
eyes follow.
Everywhere the woman goes,
people whisper.
Everything the woman touches,
others abandon.

Her face is known,
Name slandered,
She can't find work
She cannot go home

No place is safe.

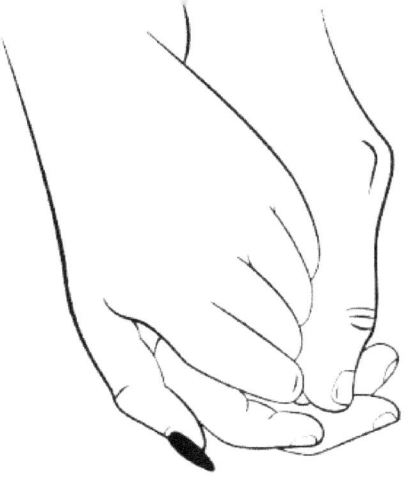

PIECES

FIRST THE EYE
   and then a foot

   It doesn't matter where she goes
   or even how she looks.

   Next, an arm
   and lastly the head

   She cannot forget the piece,
   in her bed.

   The piece that scarred her,
   and made her womb barren

   The stuff of nightmares
   that demons ensnare
   which pull and tear

and feed her despair.

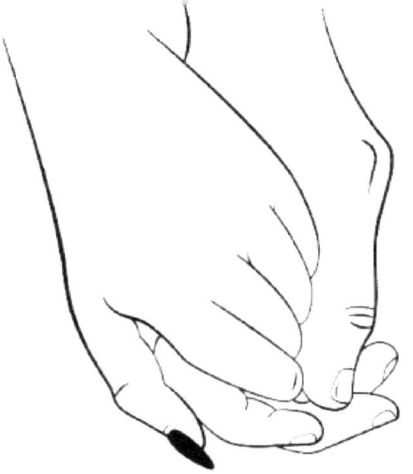

ILL

A SICKLY WOMAN
is an unhappy woman
whose energy is low,
appetite diminished,
who doesn't frown or smile
or play with her child.

With sunken cheeks
and withered hands
She relies on her man
to care for them

And every night
she stays in her room
fearing her departure
will end in her doom.

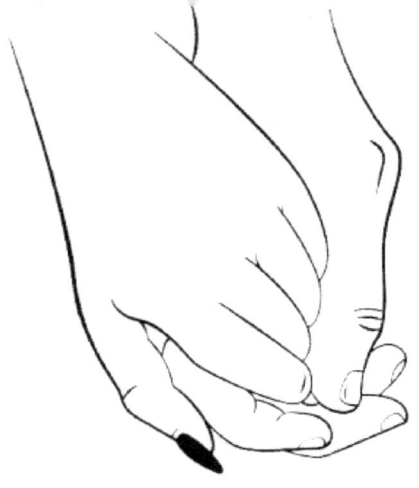

Madness

"We're doing everything we can"
   Is what they say,
   with bags under their eyes
   and frowns on their faces.

"Are you okay?"
   They always ask
   with pity in their brows
   and alcohol in their flask.

"You should see someone"
   They advise
   hands counting money
   placing on their disguise.

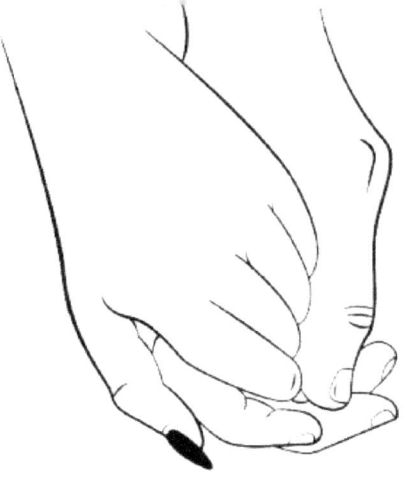

MONEY

Layers of snow
   build on the ground
   turning the loud city
   into a quiet town.

   Unsteady hands
   pry open the mail
   The tired, withered, woman
   gives out a wail.
   On her statement in a settlement
   money for her loss
   her prayers have been answered.

   Yet, at a cost
   Bloody money
   for bloody work
   The pay of a dead man
   There's no turning back

from the rage of his kin.

Fortune beyond belief
ready to be cashed
But if accepted,
her conscience will be dashed.

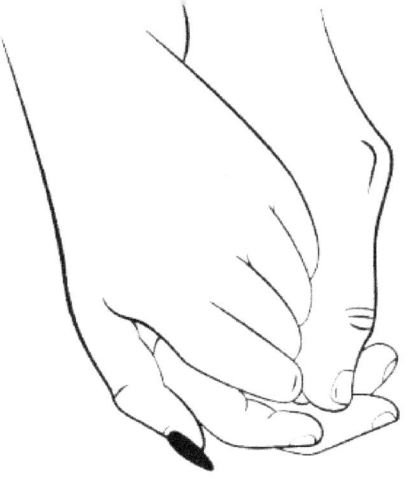

LIES

A FAKE WIFE IS first
   then a mother
   then the father
   all these others who come
   and try to bother
   for the money
   The life insurance claim

   But they are ignored
   or plainly,
   turned away
   right at the door.

Repetitious Loops

I STUMBLE
   into you
   Forever and ever
   Even after life.

   You manage to appear
   here but not here.
   It's my money now.

   I forgive your sins
   I will repay your parents
   pay off my home
   And gift my family.

   It's my money now,
   and I should do as I please
   forgive your trespasses
   And visit you at your grave .

You would approve,
for now I feel
just like you

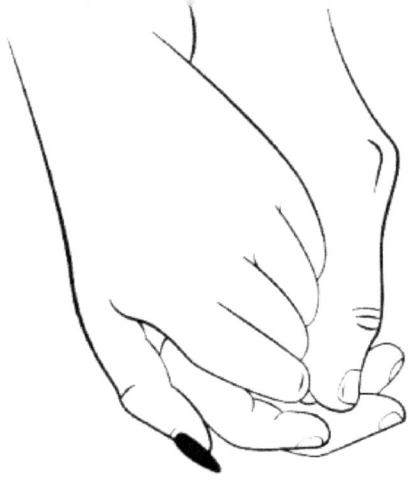

A Fire

Some sparks are a surprise,
accidental...

But some sparks burn with a *fury*
catch on the grass
splinter the glass
devour everything in sight.

They start out of spite
and grow with **might**
grazing over life

Some sparks
catch on fire.

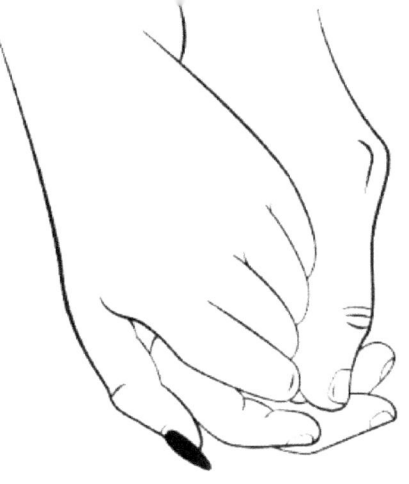

SURPRISE

EVEN WITH NO HOME
   or any place to run

   It would take anyone by surprise
   when they open their eyes
   and there sits two lines
   One faint, but clear as day
   The other strong, and for which they pray.

   A smile cannot capture true joy,
   nor true fear
   For what will they do
   when the child
   is here?

A Means To An End

AT THIRTY, YOU'VE SEEN something

    I've never seen anything beyond my own mind
    Nothing beyond my recognition
    Not even death can surprise one who's come so close.

    If you find yourself in these words
    Then open your eyes
    Because you cannot see
    You cannot feel
    You do not know

    How to
    trust in yourself
    or
    How to
    Flee.

But it's okay to be numb,
if it hardens you
guards you
until you break
down the blocks
on your soul
like me.

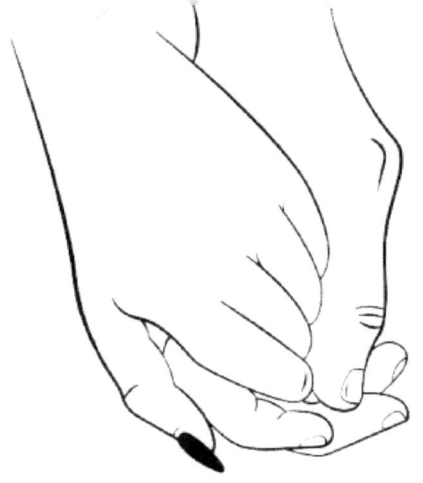

WARFARE

IN SOME BOOKS THE damsel's in distress
  In some books the myths become reality
  In some lives the damsel becomes the hero
  In some lives the lies are just the truth
  but hidden
  behind colorful words,
  or a break in breath
  held secret by death
  and taken eerily slow

  Until it's sudden
  and red
  and bright so that it hurts
  It squeezes, tightly

  But mostly
  leaves you empty
  at warfare with yourself

ENOUGH

ONE IS JUST ENOUGH

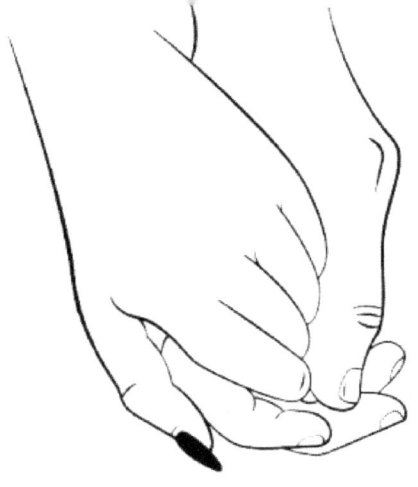

AGAIN

"MOMMY"
   Is hard to hear
   when you've lost so much

   "Mama"
   Is hard to hear
   and just not enough

   "Mom"
   Is hard to hear
   but for my sanity

   Say it again

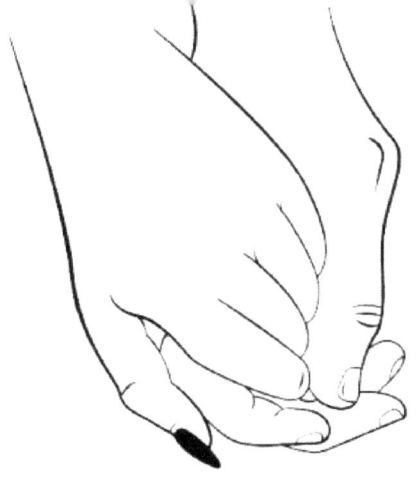

OBSESSION

BABIES.
    The word opens a chasm
    The hands' spasm
    Reaching
    Grabbing
    Tapping
    Laughing
    Delirious with doubt
    That her body has failed
    To mother
    another
    child.

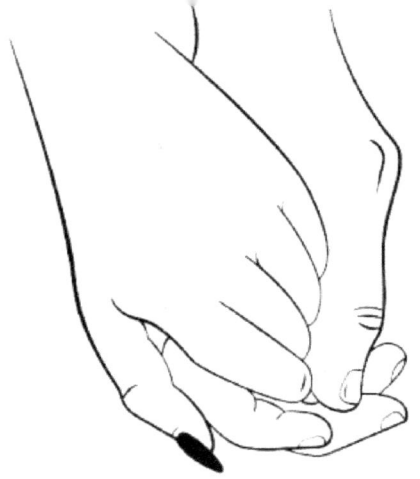

Loss

IN A HOME
>there is always one.
>Whose shadow's so dark
>they block out the sun.
>Whose grief is so strong
>life crumbles around it
>Like petals of a dead
>rose.

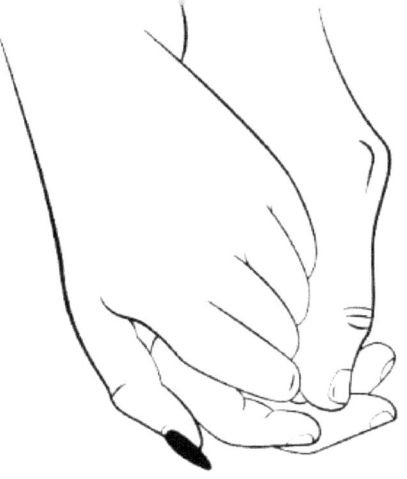

BOXES

THE DOOR
- at the end of the hall
- Stands tall
- and proud
- But remains
- *E m p t y*

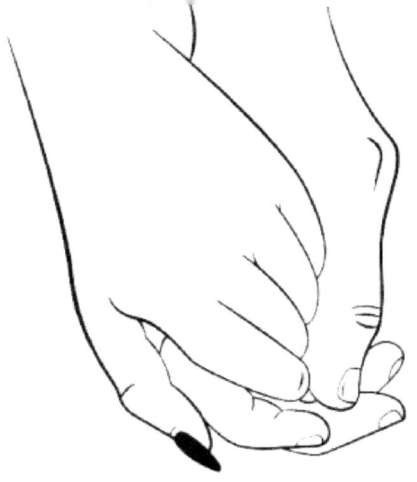

Cycles

IT MUSTN'T BE TRUE
    The blood,
    old and new
    It crusts
    and pusses
    and bleeds through.

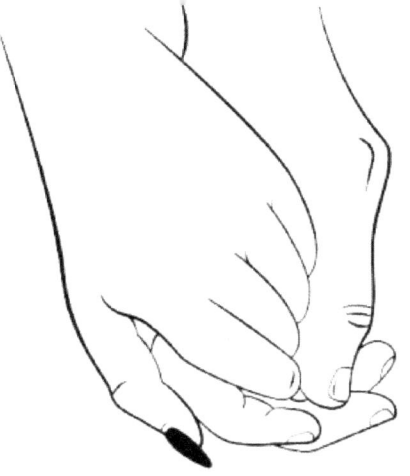

Explode

THE WALLS SHAKE AND grate against themselves
   Ticking like a bomb
   A silent alarm
   That sounds on and on
   Until the sound is just
   gone.

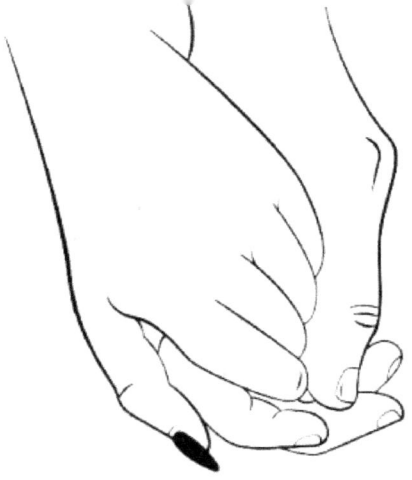

Numb

Without
   something
   to calm her soul

   She drifts through life

   Numb to the death
   her sadness creates
   Numb to the whispers
   her form produces
   Numb to the room
   and how cold it's become.

A Spark Of Hope

With a sickness comes
   a spark of hope
   and like magic
   it is there.
   Thinner than a hair
   and barely fair
   Two lines answer
   a prayer.

Again We Move

Where the air is fresh
   and opens our breast
   With pollen that traces our bodies,
   dirt that clings to our feet,
   and water that seeps
   into our ironclad souls,
   deep into our bellies
   and down to our toes,
   Again we move
   to a new home.

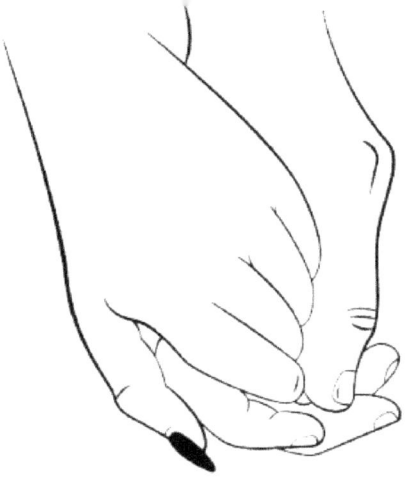

Fresh Air

O<small>N A POCKET OF</small> land
   so dearly secluded
   It is not included on any map.
   Surrounded by trees
   Nourished by bees
   And has the sweetest
   Freshest
   A i r

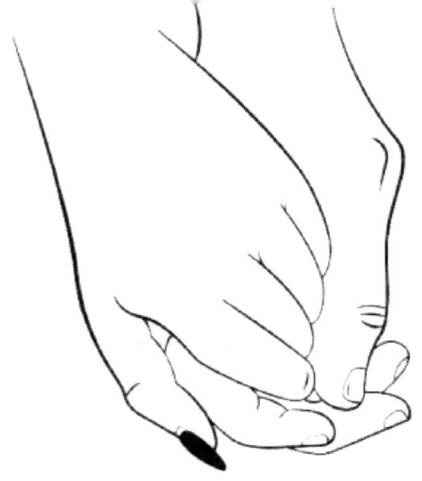

JOY

TREMORS
Shake my foundation
Erupt into my cycle
of life

A joy like no other

Small
Precious
Blessed

The way you breathe
for me
Makes it all
OKAY

I'm fine
As long as you are

here
my dear
Rainbow child.

Quickly Falling

For you
>I rise
>For you
>I dream
>For you
>I overcome anything.

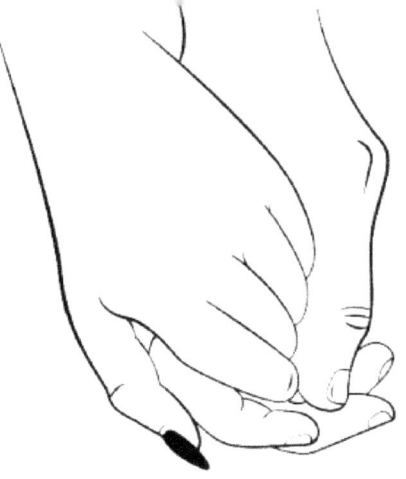

Natural

LIKE A MOTH TO a flame
or water to a hurricane
I came to life
stepped up
to become more
than myself.

Your mother
Your teacher
Your guardian

Thank you
for saving me.

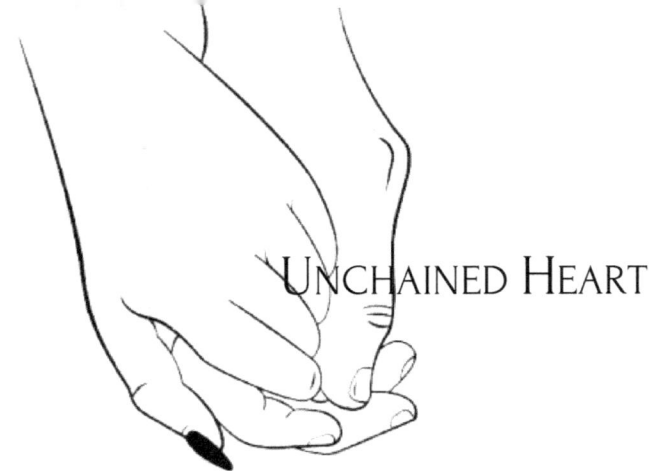

Unchained Heart

Rapidly I...
    flap my wings
    soaring high
    through the clouds
    above the blue
    ascend to you
    like a balloon.
    My unchained heart
    loves so graciously
    Beyond words
    Beyond death
    Beyond my mind's comprehension.

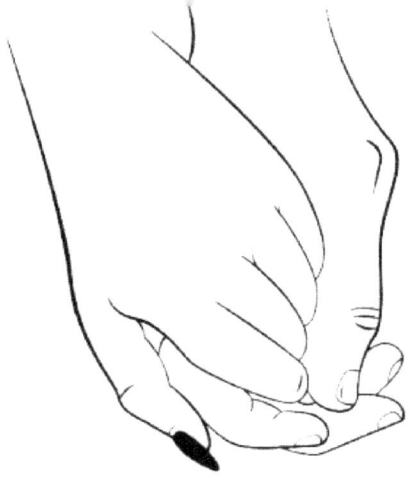

Uncaged

Run
    arms outstretched
    voice raised to the sky
    with the sky reaching back

    See beyond mortality
    See the endless trees
    and lazy river
    the fluffy white clouds
    and bright flowers
    See yourself uncaged
    in nature's embrace.

Wild and Free

Grow
    tall like trees
    strong like bears
    smart like bees
    fast like hares

    Stay steady
    and quiet
    Don't move
    Not yet
    NOW

    Pounce onto the world
    like a hunter
    does its prey

Beyond This Home

"What's beyond the trees?"
   I know you will ask
   with eyes so honey brown
   and as big and as round
   as your dad's.

   "What does the world look like?"
   I know you will ask
   with skin so deeply brown
   and a crooked frown
   that mimics my own.

   "Where does the river lead?"
   I know you will ask
   Standing at its bed
   you'll dip in your head
   and scare away the fish.

"What's beyond our home?"
I know you will ask
with child-like curiosity
hopeful and honestly.
So how shall I answer?
*"A scary but **beautiful** world"*

AND LIVE we shall.

Also By

The Limpid Series
Black Or With Sugar?
Windchimes and Sirens
Murder Bird
Light and Sweet

Other Poetry Collections
Mournful Lover

JAZMIN GALLOWAY started writing poetry in the third grade. With decades of practice came many life changes, achievements, losses, and mistakes. Galloway uses her life experiences and dreams of life to come, and life that has passed, to inspire her poetry. You can find her on Facebook and Instagram @jazminsbooks

www.ingramcontent.com/pod-product-compliance
Lightning Source LLC
Chambersburg PA
CBHW071251070526
44583CB00017B/2424